MY HOLIDAY STORY BOOK

BY MORRIS EPSTEIN

Illustrated by Arnold Lobel

KTAV PUBLISHING HOUSE INC.

To
Guita Eve
and
Sherry Lee

For your children's sake I give you the Torah.
—Rabbi Meir

SBN 87068-368-3

CONTENTS

Fish For Shabbat

Gita wrinkled up her nose and said firmly:

"I won't eat it."

There was no changing her mind. When Gita said something and wrinkled her nose squirmy-like at the same time, she meant business.

Mother looked at her across the table and said: "Eat the fish, Gita. It's good for you." And Father said: "Mother is right. And it tastes good, too." And Gita's little brother, Jerry, who was six years old, which meant that he was two years younger than Gita, said: "Yum, yum!"

Jerry and Father had come home from the synagogue a short while ago. The table was decked in gleaming white, and the silver candlesticks held the candles which Mother had blessed just before dusk. She had covered her head and said the Hebrew words for: "Blessed art Thou, O Lord our God, King of the Universe, Who hast made us holy by Thy commandments and commanded us to kindle the Sabbath lights."

When Father and Jerry returned from the synagogue, they greeted Mother and Gita with a hearty "Good Shabbat!" Father poured red wine from the fat wine-bottle and said the Kiddush, a beautiful prayer which reminds us how holy the Sabbath is.

After that, Father recited the Ha-Motzi, the blessing over bread, and cut the twisty Sabbath loaf, the hallah. He gave everyone a generous slice.

"Is anybody hungry?" Mother then asked with a grin. "I am!" said Father. "Me, too," said Jerry. And Gita? What did *she* say?

Gita said nothing.

Mother busied herself with a fork and a ladle, making sure that the golden soup was just right, and the roast chicken crisp and brown. But when she brought the tasty-looking fish to the table, Gita said:

"I won't eat it. Fish every Shabbat. I'm tired of it."

Father thought a moment, and said: "You can never tell what's *inside* a fish, Gita. Would you like to hear a story?"

Gita opened wide her big blue eyes, as if to say: "I like stories better than anything else in the world!"

"Long ago there lived a man named Joseph," said Father. "Joseph was poor, but he always saved his pennies to buy the very best food for the Sabbath. Joseph had

a neighbor named Gabriel—"

"Was he poor, too?" interrupted Gita.

"No, he was rich as an emperor," replied Father. "And Gabriel used to laugh at Joseph, saying:

"'I have *never* kept the Sabbath, yet *I* am rich, and *you* are poor.'

"One night Gabriel dreamt that he was about to lose all his wealth. He also dreamt that Joseph would soon be rolling in gold and jewels.

"Next morning, Gabriel awoke in great fright. He opened his treasure-chest and poured all his diamonds and emeralds and rubies onto the table.

"'I'll sew these gems into my high turban,' he thought. 'And then I'll sail away on a ship. I'll put *half* the world between me and Joseph!'

"On the high seas, a terrible storm broke

loose without warning. Enormous waves splintered the decks and the tall mast shuddered as though a giant were shaking it. Suddenly a gust of wind whipped Gabriel's turban off his head.

"'My turban!' he cried. 'All my worldly goods!'

"With a great gulp, the waves swallowed Gabriel's precious turban. On the very next Thursday, Joseph trudged as usual to the market-place. He stopped at the fish-dealer's.

"'I'll take that nice fish,' he said, pointing to a big fat one with shining scales. Then he added, sighing, 'Even though it will cost me my last penny.'

"'A good choice, Joseph,' said the fish-dealer in a gruff voice. 'Really fresh. The fishermen had quite a catch. All the fish were driven in by a very monster of a storm.'

"Joseph brought the fish home. 'What a large and lovely fish!' exclaimed his wife. She cut it open and then she caught her breath. 'Joseph, look!' she said.

"In the fish lay a raggedy turban, and

in the turban nested a glittering assortment of priceless jewels.

"Joseph and his wife thanked God for their great fortune, and they never were in need for the rest of their days."

When Father had finished telling the story, Gita stared thoughtfully into space. She considered how nice the Sabbath was, and how pleasant the Sabbath songs they soon would sing. She pictured going to the synagogue on Sabbath morning and listening to the Torah being read and saying the prayers together. And she thought of Havdalah, the prayer separating the Sabbath from the rest of the week. Father would recite Havdalah when the first three stars appeared in the heavens on Saturday evening, using red-and-white twist candles, a spice-box and a glass of wine. Yes, the Sabbath was really a wonderful day, from beginning to end.

Gita tucked her napkin into her blouse, and began to eat the portion of fish that had been set before her. Then she paused.

"Jerry," she said solemnly.

"What, Gita?"

"You know that man Joseph, the one Daddy was telling us about. And that fish he brought home for Shabbat. The one with the jewels, I mean. He *really* had 'gefillte fish' for Shabbat, didn't he?"

The Boy's Prayer

The days before Rosh Hashanah were busy ones for Gita and Jerry. They helped Mother with her shopping. Mother had a list and Gita checked off the items. The list included rosy autumn apples to munch on, and sweet honey for father to dip bread into and say:

"May the New Year be as sweet as this honey."

Gita loved Rosh Hashanah, the Jewish New Year. The house was full of fragrant flowers and the table was set with the best linen and silver. The synagogue, too, looked scrubbed and fresh and more holy than ever. The Ark was covered with a white silk curtain instead of the usual dark one. And the shofar, the curved ram's horn, was brought out of its velvet bag, ready to be used for the long, loud blasts blown on the New Year.

Outside, the red and purple fall leaves had begun to flutter to the ground. It was a brisk Sunday afternoon just before Rosh Hashanah and Gita was carefully writing New Year cards to her relatives and

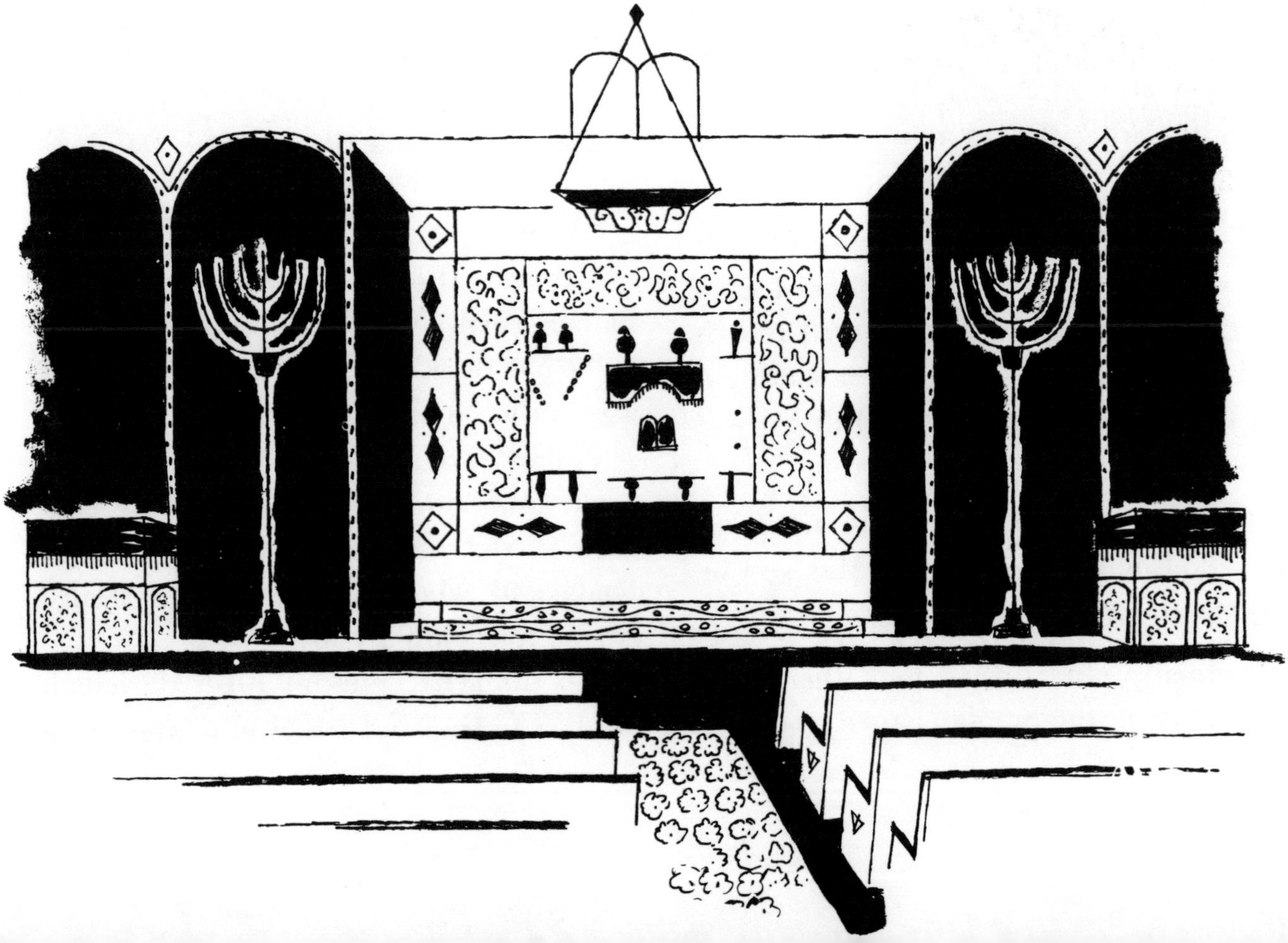

friends. Father had written out a sample for her. She slowly copied it, her tongue peeking out of the corner of her mouth. Jerry was very busy too. He licked each envelope, put the New Year card into it and sealed it. Then he placed a stamp on the envelope and made certain that it was pasted tight.

Gita wrote: *L'shanah tovah tikatevu*, and the English translation, "May you be inscribed for a happy year."

Suddenly Gita turned to Father, who was enjoying the Sunday paper.

"What does 'inscribed' mean, Daddy?"

"It means 'written in'," said Father.

"Written in — in what?" Gita kept on.

"In the Book of Life," answered Father, rustling his newspaper a little.

"What Book of Life?" asked Gita. She was not to be put off *that* easily.

Father gave up. He put the newspaper down and said, "The Book of Life contains all the names of those who do good deeds and who will enjoy good health during the coming year.

"In the synagogue on Rosh Hashanah we pray to God and ask Him to grant us a good year of life and happiness. And on Yom Kippur, the Day of Atonement, it is decided in Heaven who shall live and who shall be happy. Yom Kippur falls about a week after Rosh Hashanah and is the most solemn holy day of the whole year."

"But, Daddy," said Gita, a quiver in her voice, "I can only say *some* of the prayers. And Jerry, why, he's only *six*. What about us, Daddy?"

Father held back a smile. He pulled Gita and Jerry close to him.

"Children," he said, "your few prayers are just as important as anyone's. Why, once there was a little boy who had a whistle, and . . ."

"A story!" cried Gita, and clapped her hands.

"A story!" echoed Jerry gleefully.

"Very well, a story it shall be," said Father with a grin.

"There once was a great rabbi named the Baal Shem Tov, the Master of the Good Name. He was known for his kind-

ness to all living beings, human and animal alike. One year, on the eve of Yom Kippur, all the townspeople gathered in the synagogue. The Baal Shem Tov, whom everyone called the 'Besht' for short, stood near the Ark. Slowly he chanted Kol Nidre, the beautiful prayer said only on Yom Kippur Eve.

"The Besht said the Kol Nidre prayer three times. Then, with tears streaming down his cheeks, he began the prayer a fourth time. The congregation was shocked. Everyone knew that Kol Nidre was only said three times! Why was the Besht chanting it *four* times?

"In the meantime, a Jew from the village and his little son had entered the synagogue. They stood in the back. The man was ashamed of himself because he had never taken the trouble to teach the boy any Hebrew, and the boy could not pray.

"But the boy wanted *so much* to pray. He wanted to tell God how unhappy he was because he was different from the other boys in the synagogue.

"Again and again he opened his mouth, but not a word of prayer came out. Suddenly, the boy pulled a reed whistle out of his pocket. His father said, 'Put that away. One may not whistle in a holy place.'

"The boy pleaded with his eyes. His

father swallowed the lump that was in his throat and looked away, blinking. He felt sorry for his son. Then the boy put the whistle to his lips. In the hushed synagogue, he blew long and hard upon his whistle.

"The congregation grew very angry. Several men rushed up. They wanted to chase the boy out. At that moment, the Besht raised his hand for silence and said:

" 'All evening I have prayed hard so that our sins might be forgiven. But I felt that my prayers were not being heard. When this little boy blew on his whistle, a strange thing happened. I knew at once that he had caused our prayers to be accepted by God. Because of this boy who has never wronged anyone, we shall all be inscribed in the Book of Life.' "

Father paused and looked at Gita and Jerry. "You see, children," he said, "*how* we pray is not most important. What *is* important is that we pray as best we can. We must have a pure heart and a clean soul. Always remember the story of that little boy. Especially on Rosh Hashanah and Yom Kippur."

Gita straightened Father's tie and looked right into his eyes. "Daddy," she said, "would you please take me to the Public Library tomorrow?"

"Certainly," Father replied with a look of surprise. "Is there any book in particular you want to read?"

"Yes, Daddy," said Gita. "I'd like to read the Book of Life."

Gita
Meets Some Friends

Never was the synagogue so crowded. It was Simhat Torah Eve. All the Torah scrolls, clothed in their beautiful mantles, were taken out of the Ark. Around and

around the synagogue they were carried—once, twice . . . seven times. Gita and Jerry and all the other pupils of the Hebrew school marched along with the grownups. They held high their little flags topped by shiny freckled apples.

The big people sang and clapped their hands and celebrated. Gita and Jerry paraded and ate the chocolate bars given out by the Principal. Tomorrow night the holiday would be over. In the morning, the reading of the Torah would come to an end and would be begun all over again from the very first word "Berayshis."

At last, the dancing and the singing drew to a close. Gita and Jerry went home with Mother and Father. When they got into the house, Mother looked at the kitchen clock. "My it's *very* late," she exclaimed. "Into bed with you, Jerry and Gita."

The children undressed, washed, and brushed their teeth. They said their prayers with Mother and tumbled into bed. "I bet I'll be asleep in one minute," said Gita, yawning. "I bet I'll be asleep in one second," cried Jerry, curling up like a caterpillar.

But somehow, Gita couldn't find a comfortable spot. She tossed and turned. She rolled over and called softly, "Jerry!" But Jerry was fast asleep. Gita tried lying on her back, then on her stomach, and then on her side, but it was no use. She lay there a long, long, time, staring into the dark. . . .

Suddenly she heard a faint scratch at the door. She sat up in bed and beheld a most amazing procession marching into the bedroom. First came a fat yellow etrog, with two twinkling eyes and a pair of stubby legs. Next strode a lanky lulav, with a long face and a pointy skull. He was followed by three myrtle twigs and two willow branches, rustling in a whispery sort of way. A cluster of five willow twigs,

forming a hoshana, entered and curtsied to Gita. Bringing up the rear was a stocky sukkah, which squeezed and huffed and puffed until it just managed to get through the doorway.

All the visitors formed a neat line and looked to the sukkah for a sign to begin. He nodded, and they all said, "Hello, little Gita!"

Gita was so startled that she had to open her mouth twice before anything came out. "Wh-what are *you* doing here?" she finally blurted.

"We're very sad," said the lulav with the long face. "And we've come to make a request. But first, let us introduce ourselves."

"I-I know who you are," said Gita, rubbing her eyes in wonder. The visitors did not even seem to hear her and went right on talking.

"I'm the sukkah," said the stocky one in a deep voice. "I remind everyone of the forty years of wandering of the Israelites

in the desert. After they left Egypt, you know, they lived in booths like me. And later, in Palestine, they built booths every Sukkot. They put twigs on me for a roof, so that they could see the stars in heaven shining through. And they decorated me with fruits and vegetables and thanked God for the fine harvest He had given to them. They brought the lulav in to me. . . ."

"I'll speak for myself, thank you," broke in the lanky lulav. "Each day of Sukkot, I, a noble palm branch, am waved to the north, south, east and west, to show that God rules everywhere. I am carried around the synagogue by all the men . . ."

"And so are we!" chimed in the fat etrog and the myrtle twigs and the willow branches. "We are the hadassim and the aravot."

"All of us, except the sukkah, represent the *Arba Minim*, the 'four kinds' of growing things," said the etrog. "I am like the heart, without which man cannot live. The lulav is the spine, the myrtle is the eye,

and the willow leaves are lips. We declare that a human being ought to serve God with all his soul and body."

"Ho, there, what about me?" cried the cluster-of-five-willow-twigs. "I'm important, too! I'm the hoshana. On Hoshana Rabbah, people strike me on a bench till my leaves fall off. I remind them that just as leaves fall and grow again, so God always gives people life and new hope. And I want to say . . ."

"Stop! Stop! cried Gita, holding her hands to her ears. "*I* know *who* you all are. I learned *all* about you in Hebrew school. And Daddy uses you, and . . . and . . . But, won't you please tell me *why* you are here?"

"Well, as my friend said," remarked the sukkah, "we have a request. Sukkot and Shemini Atzeret and Simhat Torah are almost over. Where shall *we* be the day after tomorrow? I, for one, will be demolished!

"Our request is — can't you please keep us with you?" pleaded the sukkah. We want to stay all year round!"

"Yes!" all the visitors cried in a chorus. "*We want to stay with you!*"

"You poor things!" said Gita, full of sympathy for them. "I love you all! I'll take care of you. I'll take care of you! I'll . . ."

Suddenly Gita felt a hand shaking her. She opened her eyes and found Mother standing over her bed.

"Gita!" said Mother. "Wake up, dear. Why are you shouting so? It's morning. Jerry's been up for more than an hour. Don't you want to go to synagogue with Daddy?"

Gita blinked. The sun was streaming in through the window. Then she remembered her visitors. "Mother!" she cried. "What's going to happen to the etrog and lulav and everything after Sukkot?"

"Why," said Mother, "We'll take the

sukkah apart and put it neatly into the cellar. We'll put the etrog into its soft nest of straw and Daddy will keep it along with the spices when he says the Havdalah on Saturday nights. And the lulav will stand tall and straight in the corner of the sun-parlor."

"But—will they *like* that?" asked Gita. "Will they be happy?"

"What a strange question!" exclaimed Mother. "I suppose they *will*. They've done their job and we have treated them carefully. I can't very well *ask* them though, can I?"

Just then, through the open bedroom door, Gita spied Father's tall lulav, standing in the corner of the sun-parlor. A gust of wind blew in through the screened half-open window. And the lanky lulav rustled and quivered, his leaves scraping against each other, saying "*y-z-z, y-z-z, y-z-z!*"

"Look, Mommy, look! The lulav is saying 'yes.' They will be pleased! They *really* will!"

Mother said, "Wonderful, dear. Now won't you get dressed?" And Gita did, thinking, "Golly, sometimes parents just *don't* understand the most important things of all!"

The Old Dreidel

Everything in the house was topsy-turvy.

Gita and Jerry were getting ready for the Hanukkah play. The play would be presented that evening in the Hebrew school. And there were so many things still to be done!

Mother was sitting at the sewing machine. Quick as a flash, in-and-out, out-and-in, went the needle. And then, snip-snip, went the scissors. Mother was putting the finishing touches on the costume Gita was going to wear in the play.

Father had a carton of cotton before him on the table and he was pulling off great gobs of the white, woolly stuff. He was making a beard for Jerry. Now he tried it on Jerry's face.

"Glub-glub!" said Jerry. "You covered-*glub*-my mouth!"

"That's all right," giggled Gita. "You don't have to *say* anything in your part anyway!"

"But I have two parts, smarty!" replied Jerry. "You've only got one!"

It was true. Jerry was going to be one of Mattathias' soldiers and then, later, he would pull off his beard and pretend to be the little boy who discovered the tiny flask of oil in the Temple.

Gita's part was much more important. But, after all, she was older. Gita was to be the Narrator. She would tell the story of Hanukkah before the play began.

"Would you like to rehearse your part?" asked Father. "Last chance before dinner. After that, you know, off to school we go."

"All right," said Gita. She drew herself up to her full height, looked at her audience of three and cleared her throat. "Ahem," she said.

"Our play tonight," she began, "tells the Hanukkah story. Many centuries ago,

an evil man named Antiochus became king of Syria and conqueror of Jerusalem. Antiochus thought he could destroy our religion. 'I am God,' he roared. 'The Jews shall not keep the Sabbath! They must bow down and worship our Greek idols!'

"He sent 22,000 of his best soldiers to carry out his command. Soon they had looted the Temple in Jerusalem of its holy objects. They drove grunting pigs into the Temple. They sold many women and children into slavery.

"One day, Antiochus' soldiers came to the little village of Modin. There an old priest named Mattathias surprised everyone by rebelling against the king. When he saw a pagan sacrifice being performed in the market place, he became very angry. He killed the king's officer.

"Now Mattathias had to flee. Gathering his five stalwart sons and a band of hardy men, he fled to the hills. Antiochus sent four armies against him. The evil men went down like bowling pins before the hacking blows of the Maccabees. At last, in 165 B.C.E., Judah Maccabee, the son of Mattathias, and his men recaptured Jerusalem. On the twenty-fifth day of Kislev, the Jews poured into the Temple. They cleaned it and scrubbed it.

"They could find no oil to relight the Menorah in the Temple. And then, a little boy found a small cruse of oil. They lit the lights and the oil burned for eight full days. Since that time, we have celebrated Hanukkah — which means *dedication* — for eight days. On the first night of Hanukkah, we light one candle. On every night thereafter we light an additional one until our Menorah has eight candles in a row.

"In this way, we commemorate the

Festival of Lights and the Triumph of Freedom. And because Hanukkah is such a joyous holiday, we give presents to our friends and relatives. And now — on with the play!"

Gita paused and curtsied very prettily.

Mother and Father clapped their hands and congratulated Gita. Only Jerry remained silent.

"Don't you think Gita did a swell job?" asked Father.

"Sure," Jerry said. "Only . . . only she left out one thing. She didn't say that we play dreidel on Hanukkah!"

"Oh, silly!" cried Gita. "That's a *new* game. The Maccabees didn't play dreidel!"

"Now, hold on a minute, Gita," Father said. "I wouldn't be so sure of *that*. In fact there's an old story which says that the Hanukkah top *was* invented during the time of the Maccabees."

"Tell us!" Gita and Jerry exclaimed.

"Well, it's a very short legend, really. When Antiochus ruled Palestine, he did not permit the Jews to study the Torah. *You* told us that, Gita.

"To escape the king's spies, our ancestors would meet in hidden places. While one person acted as a lookout, the rest would study our Torah by heart. If sol-

diers were heard approaching, the lookout would cry out a warning. The group would quickly separate and hurry away through back doors and buried passages.

"One day, someone thought of a dreidel game to fool the king's men. They kept a top on the table. If a soldier managed to slip by the lookout, all he would see was a group of Jews gathered together to play a game. In that way, the little Hanukkah dreidel saved many lives.

"Later on, the letters nun, gimel, hay and shin were placed on the dreidel. Do you know what they stand for, Gita?"

"Yes," said Gita. "Nays Gadol Hayah Sham — A Great Miracle Happened There."

Suddenly Mother poked her head out of the kitchen. "Did I hear someone say something about saving lives?" she asked with a smile.

"That's right," said Father.

"Well I'd like to save four right now. I've just whipped up a stackful of potato latkes. Anybody care for some?"

There was a mad scramble for the kitchen, where a plate piled high with crusty, delicious latkes stood temptingly on the table.

"Mom," said Jerry, "you just made the fastest miracle I ever heard of!"

Gita Asks A Riddle

"I've got a riddle," said Father. Gita and Jerry looked up from their card game of "Old Maid." Jerry was glad to stop because Gita was winning as usual.

"Ask me!" cried Gita. "Ask *me!*" echoed Jerry.

"I'll ask both of you," Father said. "Now listen carefully. What was Adam and Eve's telephone number?"

There was a pause as the children stared blankly at Father. "Give up?" asked Father. "Give up," said Gita. "Me too," said Jerry.

"281 *APple,*" chuckled Father.

"Huh?" said Jerry.

"I get it," cried Gita. "*Two ate one apple!* That's a good one, Daddy. Ask us another!"

"All right, I will. How about this one: If I were a tree, what would you say to me today?"

Father did not get a chance to answer. Mother had tiptoed in from the kitchen. She held a bowl of fruit and other goodies. And she answered, "Happy New Year! Because, my dears, today is Tu Bi-Shevat, the New Year of the Trees. Let's celebrate!"

Quick as a wink, Mother was surrounded by the family. Soon they were munching almonds, and hard-as-nails bokser, the fruit that grows on carob trees, and figs and other delicious fruits.

"Yes, indeed," said Father, chewing into a fig, "why shouldn't trees and plants have their own New Year? They're alive and growing, just like us human beings! I once even heard of a tree that celebrated a real birthday!"

"With a cake and candles?" asked Jerry, wide-eyed.

"Not ex-*actly*," laughed Father. "After all, it was only in a story."

'Oh-h-h, a story!" cried the children.

"I guess I'd better tell it," sighed Father, making believe he really didn't want to, even though the whole family knew he loved to spin a yarn.

"Well, gather round and listen closely. This is a legend about an almond tree in Israel. All winter she stood in the orchard, cold and sad. One day, a wind wafted by and whispered to all the trees, 'Tomorrow is the birthday of the almond tree.'

"A tiny bird heard the whisper. The bird flew to the almond tree and perched on a branch. 'Tomorrow is your birthday, almond tree. I'm going to call all my friends and we shall celebrate. Chirp, Chirp!'

"Then a bee flew over and buzzed, 'Tomorrow is your birthday. *And* it's Tu Bi-Shevat. I'm going to z-z-zoom to the hive. All the bees will come to your birthday party.'

"She buzzed away and the tree stood sad and silent. 'Oh dear,' she thought, 'all those guests will come and I shall be so plain, without leaves or blossoms.'

"At last night fell, and all the trees fell asleep. Except the almond tree. She was very restless and rustled her bare branches sadly.

"At about three in the morning, the angel of flowers alighted in the orchard. He was dressed in fragrant green, with white buds and delicate blossoms.

" 'Not asleep, almond tree?' he asked in surprise. The tree told the angel her pitiful story. 'Don't worry,' said the angel. 'I promise that you will have a lovely party dress to wear for your birthday. Now get some rest. Good night!'

"The tree heaved a sigh of relief and fell asleep at once. The angel quickly bent over her and kissed each branch gently. On each branch, as if by magic, beautiful blossoms sprang out, all white and pink.

"Next morning, when the almond tree awoke, she was amazed to see all her finery. All the trees roundabout compli-

mented her and said, 'My, how lovely you look!' and 'Happy Birthday!'

"Then the birds came and the bees soon after. How they twittered and buzzed and fussed over that tree! 'B-z-z-!' sang the bees, and 'Tweet, Tweet' shrilled the birds. 'What a beautiful almond tree.'

"On that day there was not a prouder nor a happier tree in all the wide world!"

Mother and Gita and Jerry clapped their hands as a good audience should. But something bothered Gita, and she said, "If the New Year of the Trees comes in January or February, wouldn't it be too *cold* for the almond tree to blossom?"

"Aha! A *very* good question, young lady," said Father, "for which I will reward you with one plump fig. Now, does anybody here know the answer?" He looked around at his audience.

"I do, kind sir," laughed Mother. "*That* tree was growing in Israel. When we're still wearing our winter coats in the United States, spring is just beginning in Israel. And Tu Bi-Shevat, which really means the fifteenth day of the Hebrew month of Shevat, is an old Jewish custom that began in ancient Palestine. It marks the start of Israel's spring season."

"Cor-rect!" exclaimed Father. "A crunchy piece of bokser for you, my dear! You know, I think the nicest thing about this holiday is that it was so chock-full of meaning in olden times and has a new meaning today which is *just as* important."

"What do you mean by that, Daddy?" asked Gita.

"Well," said Father, "Our forefathers in Eretz Yisrael realized the value of trees and plants. They even had a custom of planting trees to celebrate the birth of children. When a baby girl was born a cypress tree was planted for her. When a boy was born a cedar tree was planted. The trees grew with the children. When

the children married, branches of their trees were used to make the marriage canopy.

"When our people had to leave Palestine, we took our holidays with us. Even in cold northern countries, on Tu Bi-Shevat, families would gather and eat all kinds of Palestinian fruit.

"Today, Tu Bi-Shevat has a new meaning. We help the Jewish National Fund plant little saplings in Israel, so that the Jewish State can once more become a land of shady forests and fruit-bearing orchards."

Gita pressed her nose against the frosty window-pane and gazed at the snow-laden tree in front of the house. "Daddy," she said, "you told us that trees are alive, just like human beings."

"That's right," nodded Father. He wondered what was coming next. He did not have long to wait, for Gita said, with a smile in her voice, "*I* always thought that a tree was just like a dog."

"Like a *dog?*" said Father.

"Sure," replied Gita. "Don't they both have a bark?"

"That'll teach me to ask riddles," said Father, relaxing in his easy chair.

Father's Secret Invention

"Is Daddy going to take us in the car?" asked Gita. She and Jerry were struggling into their coats. Mother had prepared a basketful of gifts, each neatly tied with a bright ribbon. They were Shalah Manot gifts, and Gita and Jerry had the important task of bringing the presents to friends and relatives of the family who lived in the neighborhood. Each year Father had gone with the gifts, with Gita and Jerry in tow, like little tugboats following a great ocean liner. But this year, Gita was old enough to bear the responsibility, and she was very proud.

"I'll ring the doorbell," she declared, "and I'll say, 'We've brought some Shalah Manot presents for you!' "

"And I'll say Happy Purim!" chimed in Jerry, hopping merrily on one foot.

"But won't Daddy take us in the car?" Gita repeated.

"I'm afraid not," said Mother. "He's very busy in his study and can't be disturbed. And *I* can't take you either, else I'll never get these Hamantashen done. So you just run along—"

"What's Daddy *doing?*" asked Jerry.

"He's making a — no, I promised I wouldn't tell. It's a Purim secret. You'll find out when you get back. Now, off with you both, so that I can get to work."

And Mother shooed Gita and Jerry out of the house without another word.

* * *

About two hours later, two weary children trudged into the house. Tired though they were, their faces were wreathed with smiles. Mother was resting on the living room couch, her feet tucked beneath her, when they marched in.

"Hi, Mom!" they said. "Look at what we have!" Gita pointed to the basket, which seemed as full as when they had left.

"Wasn't anybody home?" Mother asked in mock dismay.

"Sure," said Gita, "these are the presents *we* received." Just then she noticed Father. He was sitting in his favorite easy chair, holding a mysterious-looking bundle of papers in his hand.

Gita and Jerry bounded over to Father. "Tell us a Purim story!" they cried.

Father had a strange smile on his face. "Not this time," he said. "We're going to do it the other way around. If *you* can tell *me* the story of Purim, I'll do something extra special for you.

"And here's a little food for thought," said Mother, rising and taking the cover off a plateful of delightful-looking three-cornered Hamantashen. "Poppy-seed or plum-jam filled?" she asked.

"Both!" said Jerry.

"M-m-m!" said Gita, biting a corner off a Hamantash. "Where shall I begin, Daddy?"

"Why not begin at the beginning?" smiled Father. Start with 'A.' 'A' stands for—"

"—Ahasuerus!" exclaimed Gita. "He was a silly old king who lived many years ago. He thought he'd have some fun, so he threw a big party. He ordered his queen Vashti to come to the party."

"He didn't *invite* her, did he," said Father. "He *ordered* her to come." Father extended a little slip of paper to Gita. "Here, read this, Gita. I made it up while I was working on—something else today."

Gita read:

When Vashti heard her husband's order,
She thought, 'Am I but a fancy boarder?'
She arched her brows and wrinkled her nose,
And said 'Tell the King to twiddle his toes!'

Everybody laughed. "Hooray for Daddy," said Jerry. "He's a poet and he doesn't know it," said Mother, making a poem herself.

"Thank you, dear," declared Father.

"Go on, Gita. What happened next?"

"Well," continued Gita, "old Ahasuerus got very angry. He banished poor Queen Vashti. Then he decided to hold a beauty contest to choose a new wife. Of all the girls in the land, fair Esther was picked as the most beautiful. Her uncle Mordecai was *very* happy for her. And so was everybody else, except Haman—"

"Gr—GR-GR-Grog!" went Jerry's grogger. He had kept it hidden till Gita mentioned the word Haman. Now he twirled it with all his might. *"Gr-GR-Grog!"* it went.

"You'd better save your strength for

the Megillah reading in the synagogue," said Father. "Go on, Gita."

"Haman was the king's adviser and he was angry because Mordecai refused to bow to him at the palace gate. So Haman

begged old King Ahasuerus to let him destroy all the Jews. Mordecai and Esther were very upset, and asked the king to come to a little private dinner. . . ."

"Hold on," said Father. "Didn't you forget something? Remember how the king couldn't sleep one night and he ordered his diary read to him and he heard how Mordecai had once saved his life when two traitors wanted to kill him?"

"That's right," said Gita. "So he asked Haman what was the best way to honor a

person. And Haman, thinking the king meant *him*, said to dress the man in royal robes and seat him on a royal horse. And the king said: 'Fine. Do that to Mordecai!' Was Haman surprised!

"Anyway, at her private dinner, Esther told the king all about Haman's evil plot. 'Why are you so upset about these Jews?' said the king. 'Because I am a Jewess myself,' Esther said.

"King Ahasuerus remembered how Mordecai had saved his life. And he punished Haman instead of Mordecai. On the very same day that the Jews were going to be killed, Haman was hung high up in the air. On the thirteenth of Adar, long ago."

"Excellent!" said Father. "That is why we the Jews of Shushan celebrated the next day. And that is why *we* too rejoice on the fourteenth of Adar, which is Purim, and read the Megillah, which tells the whole story.

"And now, would you like a special treat?"

"A story?" cried Gita. "No," said Father. "A game for Purim. I made it up this afternoon, while you were delivering the Shalah Manot gifts."

Now Father unfolded the mysterious-looking sheets he had been holding. The whole family sat around the dining-room table and played Father's game, which he

called "Win the Hamantash!" And when he said that Purim meant "lots" or "chances" because chances were drawn to see on which day the Jews were to be killed, Gita remarked, "I would say that Purim sure is LOTS of fun!"

* * *

Would you like to play the very same game? Here are the rules. You can have LOTS of fun, too!

Rules for
WIN THE HAMANTASH!

The Rules: You will need dice and a button or coin for each player. Throw the dice and high number starts first. Advance the number of spaces indicated by the top or bottom number of the dice, whichever you think best for you. If your marker stops on a space already occupied by another marker, the other marker must move back six spaces. If that move brings it back to a star, it moves ahead seven spaces from that star. You must move your marker on each throw, except when it is resting on the last two spaces. When you reach these spaces, you must wait until you throw a 1-6 or a 6-1 to win the game; but you may be shoved back by another marker landing on your space. The game ends when a player reaches the Hamantash!

And on this day we celebrate
The Jews' escape from a wicked fate
On Adar 14th of this year
We eat the treat that's pictured here.
At the feast Esther tells the story
Of Haman's plotting, grim and gory.
Haman filled the King's ear with false news
And terrible lies about the Jews
Sweet Esther is chosen the fairest in the land.
Mordecai refuses to bow to Haman.
START

A Just Reward

The house was full of guests. It was the afternoon before the first night of Passover. So many relatives had come to join the Seder table that the walls of the house seemed ready to burst. Grandpa and Grandma had come from the big city. And Uncle David and Aunt Sarah, who lived just around the corner. And Cousin Joseph, and Cousin Bob, and great-Aunt Miriam.

Gita and Jerry were sitting with Grandpa in the living room. Everyone else was bustling about, dressing to go to the synagogue, or setting the table. In the center of the table was the Seder Plate. On it were three matzot, a roasted meatbone, an egg, bitter herbs, haroset, and parsley.

Gita yawned and covered her mouth politely. She was just a little tired. She had helped Mother put away the everyday dishes and take out the Pesah dishes. The night before she had followed Father in the B'dikat Hametz ceremony. He had gone into every room carrying a feather and a wooden spoon.

With the feather he brushed little bits of bread onto the spoon, until the very last of the crusts that Mother had placed here and there was swept up. There was no more Hametz in the house.

Gita was glad to see Grandpa again. He was her favorite relative because, next to Father, he knew the most good stories. Grandpa had a white beard and wore glasses that always seemed as though they would slide right off his nose. When Gita was a baby, Mother told her, she would grasp Grandpa's beard with her chubby fingers and pull very hard. And Grandpa would throw his head back and roar with laughter.

"Gita," said Grandpa. "Who's going to hide the Afikomen tonight?"

"Sh-h-h!" whispered Gita. "Don't let Daddy hear you. Jerry and I are going to take it and we won't give it back until Daddy promises each of us a bicycle!"

"I want a two-wheeler!" said Jerry.

Grandpa took off his glasses and cleaned

them. "When I was a boy, I took the Afikomen and . . ."

"When *you* were a boy!" exclaimed Gita. "Did they have Seders *that* long ago?"

Grandpa grinned. "Do I look three thousand years old, Gita? Because that's how old Pesah is. It all began in the days of Moses . . ."

"I know," said Gita. "He led our people out of slavery."

"That's right, Gita. Pharaoh was the king of Egypt at that time. He was a most cruel king, too. He made our ancestors work very hard, building his mighty pyramids and palaces.

"One day Moses, a young Hebrew shepherd, was tending his sheep near a mountain called Sinai. Suddenly he heard the voice of God coming from a burning bush. God told Moses to go to Pharaoh and command him to set the Israelites free.

"But Pharaoh just laughed. So God punished Pharaoh and the Egyptians. He sent plagues upon them. The rivers turned to blood. Frogs and darkness and wild animals overran Egypt. Still Pharaoh's heart remained hard. At last God took away every first-born Egyptian son, and Pharaoh became frightened. He begged Moses to take his people out of Egypt. They left in great haste and had no time to bake real bread . . ."

"So they made matzot!" cried Gita.

"That's right," smiled Grandfather. "They ran and ran, till they reached the Red Sea. Pharaoh's troops were right behind them, so they jumped into the sea and God split the sea into two and they marched straight across, led by Moses and

his brother Aaron.

"So, you see, Passover is our festival of freedom, and we eat matzot on Pesah to remember the great miracles God did for us in those days."

A puzzled look crossed Gita's face. "Do we call it Passover because we passed over the Red Sea?" she asked.

"No," smiled Grandpa. "We call this holiday Passover, or Pesah, because God *passed over* all the Hebrews' houses when He took away the first-born Egyptian sons. None of the Hebrew sons was harmed that night.

"Since those days, we have celebrated Passover for eight days each spring beginning with the fourteenth day of the Hebrew month of Nisan. And at the Seder, we read the Haggadah, which is really a guide book for the celebration of Pesah. The youngest child asks the Four Questions . . ."

"I know," sighed Jerry. "That's me. I wish I didn't have to."

"Why do you say that?" asked Grandpa in surprise.

" 'Cause I know the answers. Teacher told us."

Grandpa smiled. "You ought to be glad you *can* ask the Four Questions. I remember a story about a little boy . . ."

"A story!" cried Gita and Jerry, clapping their hands in glee. "Tell us, Grandpa!"

"Well," said Grandpa, "as I remember it, there was once a boy named Saul. He had a wicked temper. He even scolded little birds who chirped in the trees. He said:

" 'Your chirping bothers me. I think I'll punish you!' And he did. He hurt the tongues of those birds so that they could not sing again. However, a wise old owl was watching from nearby, and the owl said:

'God's punishment is clear
Someone very dear
To you, Saul,
Will never speak at all!'

"Saul grew up and married. A little boy was born to him and his wife. The boy was very handsome . . . but he could not speak. And each Passover, when it was time to ask the Four Questions, Saul looked at his son and his eyes filled with tears.

"One Passover eve, Saul walked slowly home from the synagogue. Suddenly he heard a weak chirping coming from a barn at the side of the road.

"He crossed over and peered into the darkness of the barn. There he saw three baby birds fluttering their wings. One bird said:

'We tried to test our wings alone.
I fear I've broken a little bone!'

"Saul gently cupped the birds in his hands and started on his way. And a wise old owl, looking down from a leafy branch said:

'Saul has done a very good deed.
He's helped God's creatures in their need.
I think he's seen an end to sorrow,
He'll be gay before tomorrow!'

"When Saul arrived home, he asked his wife to feed the birds. Then he said, 'Let us sit down to the Seder. I have a strange feeling that we ought to start quickly.'

"Shortly afterwards, at the Seder table, Saul looked up. His heart was pounding. He said, 'Who will ask the Four Questions?'

"Just then, the birds began to chirp and chirp and chirp.

"And little Jacob, who had never uttered a word, opened his mouth and said haltingly:

" '*Mah Nishtanah Ha-Leilah Ha-Zeh Mi-Kol Ha-Laylot?* . . . How is this night different from all other nights?'

"Yes, little Jacob could speak again. Saul's good deed had brought forth golden fruit."

Grandpa looked at Jerry. "Did you like that story, Jerry?"

Jerry slid off Grandpa's lap.

"I sure did, only . . . only I wish there were *five* questions I could ask!"

Grandpa looked over his glasses. "Why, what would the fifth question be?"

Jerry replied, "I'd say to Daddy: the fifth question is — could I get a two-wheeler if I hide the Afikomen?"

Rabbi Akiba's Answer

Jerry came into the kitchen tugging at his pajamas and rubbing the sleep out of his eyes. He pulled Mother by the hand until she bent down and her head was close to his.

"Is Daddy sick?" he whispered. "He didn't get up to go to the office today."

Mother laughed and hugged Jerry until he was all out of breath. "No, Jerry," she said, "Daddy's fine and you're a good boy and it's Lag Be-Omer today. So Daddy thought he'd take the day off and go fishing with you!"

Jerry let loose a yip-yip of delight. What a treat! Fishing with Daddy! In a jiffy he was dressed. He said his morning prayers with Mother, ate his breakfast and even brushed his hair with extra care. Before long, Father had joined him. From the hall closet Father took a wicker basket. It

contained fishing lines and rods, hooks and shiny lures.

Before long, Father and Jerry had piled into the car. Mother leaned out of the window. "You forgot your lunch!" she called. Jerry ran pell-mell back to the house and took the package Mother had prepared. "So long Mom!" he cried and gave her a big hug and a kiss.

Off they went, smooth as anything. Soon they arrived at a lake in the mountains. Father rented a boat and stowed away the fishing gear in it. He examined the boat for leaks. He lifted Jerry carefully into the boat and stepped in himself. Then he pushed off.

Out in the middle of the lake, Father lit his pipe. He baited the hooks and then Jerry and he let their lines dangle in the clear, still water.

"If we sit quietly," said Father, "maybe a nice big pickerel will come along and bite."

Five minutes passed, then ten, then fifteen. Jerry began to yawn and fidget on the wooden slat that served as a seat. Father looked at Jerry and smiled. "Know why we're here, Jerry?" he asked.

"Sure," said Jerry. " 'Cause we're fishing."

"Right," laughed Father. "But why are

we fishing?" he asked. And he answered himself: "Because it's Lag Be-Omer. On Lag Be-Omer *all* Jews celebrate in a very special way.

"You see, many centuries ago, our ancestors fought against the cruel Romans who wanted to chase all the Jews out of Palestine. No one was allowed to study the Torah or to worship God. True, our people had a great leader. His name was Rabbi Akiba. But he grew very old and he looked for a younger man to take his place.

"He found such a man. His name was Bar Kochba. He was strong and fearless. Many Jews rallied to his side. He took only the bravest men into his army. Why, to join his troops, a young fellow had to be able to pull a tree right out of the ground while riding by on horseback!

"Bar Kochba and his followers hid in caves, prepared their bows and arrows and other weapons and then went out to fight against the wicked Romans. The enemy had many more soldiers and at last, in the year 135, more than 1800 years ago, Bar Kochba and his men were defeated.

"Jerry, that is why the days between Passover and Shavuot are not happy days in the memory of our people. They remind us of those sad times of long ago. All

except one day: Lag Be-Omer, which means the thirty-third day in the counting of the omer. The omer was a measure of grain which our ancestors harvested and brought to the Temple. On Lag Be-Omer, a terrible illness which had fallen upon Rabbi Akiba's students suddenly stopped.

"That's why Lag Be-Omer is a happy day. When I was a little boy in Europe, we would go into the woods and play bows-and-arrows and have a picnic, and listen to the Rabbi tell us stories."

Little Jerry jiggled his rod up and down. "But that's got nothing to do with fishing, Daddy," he complained.

Father threw a quick look at Jerry. "Quite a smart son I've got," he said to himself proudly. "In a way it has, Jerry," he remarked out loud. "For there's even a fish story about Lag Be-Omer."

"Tell me," pleaded Jerry.

"It's really about Rabbi Akiba," said Father. "He wasn't afraid of the Romans at all. He knew that studying the Torah was the most important thing in the world for the Jewish people. So he would meet his students in the woods and teach them secretly. But there were others who *were* afraid to be caught. For them, he had a story. He said that one day a fox was walking along the shore of a lake. Suddenly a shiny big fish slid through the water before his very eyes.

" 'My, what a nice-looking fish,' thought

the fox. 'I haven't eaten fish in a long time.' So the fox said to the fish, 'Why are you scurrying about so?' And the fish replied, 'I'm escaping from the—GLUB!—fishermen's nets!—GLUB!'

" 'Take my advice,' said the fox. 'Come ashore with me. I'll protect you and no one will be able to find you.' The fish just laughed, 'Ho! Ho! Ho! *GLUB!* That's silly advice. I'm frightened of fishermen even when I am right here in the water, where I can breathe and live. If I came out on dry land I wouldn't even be able to breathe. You *are* a foxy one!'

"Then Rabbi Akiba said to his followers, 'We Jews are like that fish. We're afraid of the enemy, but we study the Torah which is our way of life. Can you imagine how terrified we would be if we *stopped* our studies? It is in bad times like these that we must keep our Torah alive. For it is our Torah that keeps *us* alive!' "

Jerry suddenly felt a tug on his line. He pulled and pulled and suddenly—*PING!*—the line grew slack and Jerry drew in a shiny, empty hook.

"You nearly had him," said Father. "Big one, too."

"Aw, gosh," said Jerry. "That fish must've heard you telling the story about the fox!"

Father laughed and opened up the box of sandwiches Mother had prepared. And a very good lunch they had.

A New Commandment

"You know what, Mom?" said Gita, smiling her prettiest smile.

Mother looked at Gita. Now she would find out why Gita had been so silent during dinner. The family was gathered in the living room. Gita had been staring out of the window, quiet as a mouse. Mother knew that *something* was brewing in her daughter's mind. She put down her mending and said, "What is it, dear?"

"I think I ought to stop going to school. The term is almost over anyway. I could stay home and help you shop and . . . and . . ." She broke off; Father had that certain look in his eye, even though he wasn't saying anything.

Mother picked up one of Father's socks and the darning needle. "Did anything happen in school today, Gita? Anything unusual, I mean?"

"N-o-o-o," replied Gita slowly, slowly "Except . . ."

"Except what?" Father prodded.

"Except, if I go back to that old school, I'll keep my mouth tight shut and never say a single word!"

"Gita, what on earth happened?" Mother was really concerned now.

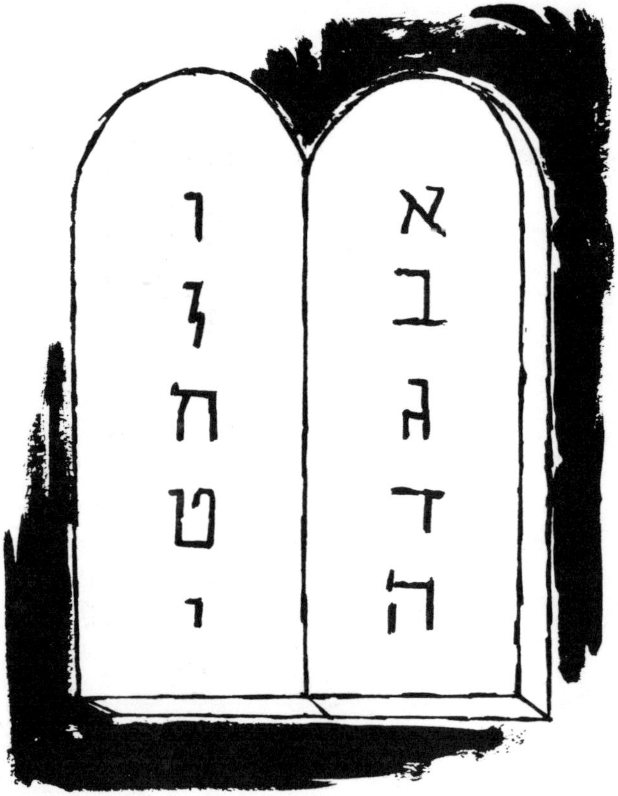

"Well," said Gita, "we were playing 'going to Jerusalem' and I told the teacher that it must be a Jewish game, because our ancestors used to go to Jerusalem three times each year. They went on Passover, Shavuot and Sukkot. We just studied it in Hebrew school, because Shavuot is coming next week."

"How wonderful!" beamed Mother, and Father relaxed, too. "The teacher must have been proud of you."

"She was *too* proud," pouted Gita. "She said that it would be very interesting for the whole class to hear about Shavuot. She said I could give a report on it tomorrow. Oh, why did I have to open my mouth!"

Father said, "I think it's a grand idea for you to tell the class about Shavuot."

"But I don't know much *about* it," complained Gita. "We didn't finish studying Shavuot in Hebrew school. All I know is that Moses brought the Ten Commandments down from Mount Sinai and . . . O-o-o-h! I've got an idea, Daddy! Why don't *you* tell me a story about Shavuot?"

Father smiled. "The *best* story is told in the Bible itself," he said. "It's very exciting, too. Can you imagine Moses leading our people through the hot desert after they had left Egypt? Just shut your eyes and think how it must have felt to face the blinding sun and burning sands each day on the long march to the Promised Land!

"Think of Moses, a proud leader, approaching Mount Sinai. He tells his people that he will climb that tall mountain to get the Ten Commandments for them. The Commandments would teach them to worship God, and to be kind and honest.

"Up he goes, higher and higher. At last he is hidden by the clouds covering the top of Mount Sinai. The people wait many days, watching for the return of their beloved leader.

"And then he comes down, holding the Two Tablets on which the Ten Commandments are written. He teaches the laws to his people, and they learn to worship one God, to be kind to each other, to be honest, to rest on the Sabbath, never to steal or kill. The children are taught to honor and obey their parents.

"That was only the beginning. When the Jews reached Eretz Yisrael, they became farmers. They built homes and tilled the soil and planted barley and wheat. They planted vineyards and olive trees, tall palms and cypress trees. In Jerusalem they built a Temple where they could worship God.

"And each year, when the grain harvest was ended, the Jews would celebrate the holiday of Shavuot. Then the farmers

would take barley and wheat and baskets of fruit that had ripened first to the city of Jerusalem as a thanks-offering to God. That is why Shavuot is sometimes called Hag Ha-Bikkurim, the Festival of First Fruits.

"Picture that scene! Jerusalem, the sun shining on its domed roofs, the pilgrims traveling from every corner of the land, on donkeys, on camels, or on foot. And then, after the celebration, returning home to till the soil and plant and reap again.

"That is the *historical* story of Shavuot. Years later, our people were forced to leave Palestine. But we have never failed to celebrate Shavuot. We decorate our homes and synagogues and schools with flowers and green branches. We eat cheese blintzes and honey cake to remind us that the Torah is sweet as honey and as nourish- as milk to those who study it and keep the Commandments."

"And we read the Book of Ruth," said Mother.

"Just like a woman, speaking up for other women," smiled Father. "Yes, we read the Book of Ruth in our synagogues. Ruth was a girl of Moab who came to Palestine with Naomi, her Jewish mother-in-law. Ruth became Jewish and accepted the Torah, just as our ancestors had accepted it. Ruth was a poor girl, and she gathered sheaves of wheat in the fields of a rich man called Boaz. Later Boaz married Ruth and they were very happy together. One of their descendants was famous King David."

"So you see, Gita," said Mother, "Shav-

uot is really two holidays in one. It is a harvest holiday and it is the Ten Commandments holiday. And we always try to make Shavuot as happy a festival as the pilgrims did when they came with their first fruits to the city of Jerusalem."

It was very quiet now in the living room. Suddenly Father rose and walked over to the window and pulled aside the curtain. "See the twinkling stars?" he said to his family. "There is a beautiful legend about the stars and the Torah.

"They have been up there in the sky for a very long time. They saw, with their eyes of light, the giving of the Torah on Mount Sinai. 'Do not give the Torah to the earthmen,' they pleaded with God. 'Let it stay with us in heaven, where all is bright and cheerful. The earth has little light and warmth, and many people there are wicked.'

"Morning came and the stars stopped twinkling. The voice of God was heard: 'The earth is cold and dark. Therefore I am giving it the Torah, so that it may be light and warm. It has no stars. The people will study the Torah and wise, learned men will bring light and wisdom to them. Then the cold dark earth will be as warm and bright as the sun and stars in heaven.'

"Then Moses went up on Mount Sinai and brought down the Two Tablets of the Law on which the Ten Commandments were written. And since that time, those very stars you see now look down upon the earth every night with sadness and longing. They long for the light of the Torah."

Mother turned to Gita and said, "Do you think you'll be able to tell the class about Shavuot now, dear?"

Gita didn't answer. She had a faraway look in her eyes. She said, "You know, Mom, if God wanted to make sure we'd be good, there really should have been *eleven* Commandments instead of ten."

Mother looked startled. "Why, what would the eleventh Commandment be?"

"*Keep the other ten!*" cried Gita, skipping out of the room.

DATE DUE

Epstein, Morris
My Holiday Story Book